MY NOT-MY SOLDIER

FENCE
BOOKS

MY NOT-MY SOLDIER

Jennifer MacKenzie

FENCE MODERN POETS SERIES

FENCE
BOOKS

Cover design by Jess Puglisi & Rebecca Wolff
Cover photo by Sami Haven
Book design by Jess Puglisi & Rebecca Wolff

Published in the United States by Fence Books
Science Library, 320 University at Albany
1400 Washington Avenue, Albany, NY 12222

www.fenceportal.org

Fence Books are printed in Canada by The Prolific Group and distributed
by Small Press Distribution and Consortium Book Sales and Distribution.

Library of Congress Cataloguing in Publication Data
MacKenzie, Jennifer [1977-]
My Not-My Soldier / Jennifer MacKenzie
Library of Congress Control Number: TK

ISBN 13: 9781934200759

First Edition
10 9 8 7 6 5 4 3 2

Fence Books are published in partnership with the University at Albany
and the New York State Writers Institute, and with invaluable support from
the New York State Council on the Arts and the National Endowment
for the Arts.

CONTENTS

Wartime Garden

Damascus

Where Are You Going

Silver Car

Where are you going Alejandro, where
Because I too would like to write
someone else's poem, gust to the margin

The gash in the turf full of pale grass, pink flowers
The bits of plastic the sea has placed just there
And the skanky brash construction paused

straggling along the ridgeline before it descends
to this feeling about blonds
that thankfully protects me from all other feelings

Thus do I maintain my sleep, a cloister drawing me
swiftly past the silver car parked
lunar by the horses. With both wings lifted

it is emitting a music of seriously sullen faces
of children posing with guns for a student photographer
who is growing increasingly nervous: his tears

and his pain thumping are making her all wet
he hopes: Do not smile, Alejandro, do not smirk
until we've passed them. Where do people come

from? from their habits. Keeping them so faithfully
all along. The brown eyes filling again
with a fierce private happiness behind the smoke

both strong forearms on the scarred table, or their bare
straw-colored skinny arms scalloped open
over the balcony railing. How his intelligence rinsed me

mixed with lust, even if thinly, tinny. Resisting
as if hatred were an excavation
I am always tunneling steadily toward my freedom

You Are Not a Bird

The officer dipping in and out of you
I guess having a good time. Excited
by a certain fast ripple in his reflection

Become an object, come on!—each one has
its lacy train. The enormous breasts
and white tiered skirt, and the relaxed gait
of her boyfriend's scapulae under his thin shirt

Their luggage rattling on brick, they are too many
They write in notebooks. Their joy sounds
like choking. Their faces so young and ruddy

and lively and stupid. You are not a bird
Each one is meaningless. They are a bird
collectively, the bird of you wasting your time
With such fair calm she surveys her work

A bearded someone rides by holding a bottle
shrieking, he seems to be enjoying his Sunday
Two dogs flanking him, tongues out. Is it tiring

to be weightless? Try helpless
Ring the bell and stand aside, they will come
to the other side of the wall and push
the wafer through on a little tray and pause

and ring the bell. Like G
shoving all his anger inside piety
as waiting for no one slowly closes

My John Wayne

Every time you crumple up a fantasy
you feel better, so why not

Make your best friend a saint, for freedom
And because you want to fuck him

The cashier with the burned hand
and bad English smiling tightly

"New skin coming! New skin
coming!"—a gleaming at the base of
the fingers like pink spit, webbing

       The truth, freedom, Sure
I say floating
inside my John Wayne body, my ghost-
buffer
            Sure it will

Under the greenwood tree
their passing hidden. Footsteps,
laughter. Is it a scar or mirror

that peculiar brightness crossing a face
involuntary. Discussing distances
and I watch them, sealing and unsealing

There is so much pressure on an ending
not to. Just like me

All Dread Is Trying To Be Kind

I am in Damascus dreaming of Vikings
The way they place their tongues
to make their songs about big sore hands
and ice and kinds of hot baths

Hey, hey, and white towels all around
The soft sea-sounds are humming
down their cold fanned grooves
The Geography Channel's helping

George is making chicken and cleaning
my coffeepot and calling me a liar
when I say I already cleaned it

All right, I am a liar. I want to swoon
into a fit of possession by sled dogs
like a premonition of an inappropriate lover
on the horizon. Hard bliss of snow

scouring at one mortal. The table is now
yellow with bananas and apples
George says he has discovered
he is old. Whiskey or wine?

Whiskey. My body very warm
with skin abounds baking all the tiny
bricks inside each wren, for pity

Pharaoh Glimmer

But you wanted to go into something
you called "a glimmer"
But it was really more like shame

But is it so different writing in pencil
It is, because the sound

You straddle the puffy blue mat
with the white line drawings of a woman
on her back. Like a Pharaoh swimming

There are the parts of your body
that are something wrong

Days you can call back into being
These are called "the future"

The unmarried sisters are washing
the cracked stone courtyard below

Jingle of women, your own
fletched No hidden in a city
you walk through foreign

without singing. Your armpits fern
-rank with lust. Your hair with smoke

Everywhere our breath bequeathed to curtains
in the quiet toss of crisis spooned
along night's back like honey, cold

Hadn't you better lay back down stung
with imagining the brides of Spartan soldiers

shorn to look like conscripts waiting
in thatched huts for dusk to fall
floating and drubbed like branches

in the dim foam of temporal bewilderment
with soft hands and rough clothes

I hang my doubt an opal
lamp among fruits. Reality
flows into all the spaces, how

strangers test our pity. Someone thinks
I am for sale and touches my arm
more insistently. How much
the limbs perceive, cooled and viva

After kissing I sit feral, waiting
for my played skin to become audible
A crouched white traitor. Ace

He is a sort of wall that I could bask on
Art thou. Yeah, well. Fetch me then

Lurking from all attempts not to think about war
end in my body white strong strange culprit

in the mirror far iron tang of well water covering
my deep heart at sea, a child lying on a carpet

I am shorn in extremis, shivering to die
I love the small field, the smell under my arms

His backache, his three of shrapnel, small
pink mole-nose of each nipple unsquashing

when I take off my bra a joy similar to panic
I felt watching him listen to music, and why

these young voices should shelter
wealthy efforts at mucho damage

Untidy with breath, gaudy with pleasure
for a little stitched while, or steadying to take

a picture of a shattered doorframe. Splinters
in silhouette. Always a train

moving west. Etc. hair messy
abject face. Ratscape. Breadspace

when rage relinquishes my chest
and fulcrum-calm of dear. Waking

I strip off my warm shirt like a country
settling doves. He doesn't know what

I mean. Well then I'm the short gray
dog trotting alongside language

An icy noon. A man enters
the restaurant, unzips his leather jacket

Can or can't go from each
bed with this cup of asking

to catch the rain inside his chest sprawled
little country crawling forward on its ribs

That's what we like you to think, we like it
when you thank us. I want to be every cage

disbelieving, blinkless. I inside the narrows
of red brick, brick dust there, of men's chests

Breaths pounded open, sun-tongs through hayloft air
Workshirts in cigarette ads, full-page, glossy

My unbound hair destroying everything
and deeply. The list of errands helps somewhat

to give me edges, but only briefly
Then an absence gashed with trees

You must take care of yourself
You must rest and work in plain gray pencil

above the unenchantable sea faithfully
consuming all entrances to itself

A face tipped up at the behest of rain. Quietly so
it is the least real voices that most own me

My Explanation of

"The true hero, the true subject, the center…is force…To define force: it is that x that turns anybody who is subjected to it into a thing."

SIMONE WEIL, *The Iliad, or the Poem of Force*

My Explanation of Poetry to My Not-My Soldier

It is finding a pattern that is truly felt
as knelt is to arched foster-blue, cool stair-tip is to fever

The forehead darkens with a sadness years later
a child doffed that does not exist, a gust
pulling a nonexistent fountain to the left

and the whole cage of beads of glitter
billows. I let the song in sometimes
to feel relief, the cold wind as the plastic sled
gulls bumping steeply downhill is a face's knife

ghosts straight through the black window ice
and out like fate smoking across the snow, no fox prints
in careful single file no snowdrops buttoned diligently

echeloned into a theory of air describing a child
with only the head missing, and the right arm

Black Mercedes Novel

I set myself to make an investigation
of silences. I find that I impede them

English of vendetta
& farms, exhausted vistas
sieved through your absence

flame in this limber ear, oiled
ghosts skidding toward cost

Piggish description stealing
more time from my body

& more than anything the trap is scorn
& complicity in being seen, fear sucked up
silvery in the roots of spectacle

I wanted someone else's lust
to pull me from sleep, streaming
with the easy beauty of it
& as a recluse I dodged & burned like a rat

I tried to address it
To find out if the peril to the soul
could be listened for

Only the acts of a painful animal
sit undissolved in sordid
messy silences which are not vigil

melting in misery fury defiance selfishness
in wanting wobbly ardor
nihil, cipher, nada scathing soft (lost
not I but) the silence are

impeccable flakes of armor
certain chances & amours attend
an inevitably unstable view

of power. Polyvocal & unsure soul
perhaps a way to stave off
history? Not I but the unheard

men are blocking the streets with fires
wind rattling a tarp out on the other dark

side of my eyelids. You, a boy carrying water
up a rocky slope, no figment I can impel

Addressing a conditional isolation
a tiny castle carved inside an egg
succumbs to the personal

Confessional Poem

I'm eating sliced cheese and cucumbers
on a smudgy mattress with no sheets

My nose isn't patrician yet but lyric still
has dead fish for eyes. Gleam w/o consequence

in the unnamable country where the lion lets more
of his apples get licked by his sacred lice

Can you find the "secret police" in that line
and seven more tilt-a-whirl tokens

There is always this mechanism skimming language from strife

Licking sweat off his upper lip, the soldier _____.

+

in poems about deer the sea and a beaten child
dreamy accusation running down the cheap middle

of nowhere motels doing Fuck-all, semi-
florid flagrant Florida orange visitor What

advantage the eye can take
from vagrancy on the insweep of

its foamy tide language folded
a long time in the shallows

I mean what we have described, have we extorted

On Hue

(for Nurdan Iskender)

It's much more exciting to fuck a devastation
of a. the torn country b. the country torn c.
musculature of bellied horses screaming

which Picasso got practicing
Guernica. Aces of pain, our
attentiveness laid (by) / played (down)

A genre modeled on omniscience
I am the voyeur tweet tweet
He stood glistening

a. like a lion b. with gray chest hair
riffling above a stolen hotel towel
recounting whores c. because

they're not going to bomb you there
in Oregon. My thighs tweet tweet not getting
bombed there

under the rapid fire of a disco ball
in a toilet stall or in a trench
begging for water

nudes of melted
bottles melted bells
tweet tweet

This artist is making a century
from Post-it notes ok
This is her puffy child's face

her watering-can eyes crying
black seeds. This is the dream

where all her teeth fall out

This is a homeless girl
This is an English woman
The English always look unhappy
but they're not it's the weather

This is a man made of strips of fabric
on his knees. This is a bomb of fabric
strips exploding over his head

But it's not a dark painting

No I don't believe that black exists
Even the sky at night isn't really
even the darkest black has some little

That's just my personal opinion
I believe every space has a gender

Small White Bed

You can say anything about women

& it will be true. This is the capacious
yes of use   The famous blue

hazard   Why women are
assigned   the grieving parts

& the prayer of Magdalena: unbind

> my debt as I
> unbind my hair

> I like the men with beards
> No you shut up

)(

One red lantern
sliding along the black

tusk track / gleam & gone
steel moment of

antler. The country came into
soldiers by the trainloads advancing

grids of fire. Later they'll place
some kind of plaque, or altar

> The Virgin Mary is the only woman
> whose feet ever touched this island

The beaten child will always know
she's special. The wound defying

all laws of logic & perspective
becomes a pedestal

)(

And who the hell are you
          I am the police

And what do you want
             Police control
             Where are you from

Ah. And if I say
the A or if I don't. Ahm

-reeka, Arab way, a jewel in the ear of
an Ethiop for Mr. William's milk opening

a silk purse from
a sow's ear. Do you have any
                antique things?
In my vagina
I dress it up a bit for him, my ancestors' Irish
face and hair, in my foreigner dinghy

soft pinks & riverweed woven torrid
pseudo-gypsy rica, arabesque my brandy
in my sober curtsey frilled with where

the tongue locates the R starts wide open
ah with the whole freedom of the opened
Then a hopeful humming stadium M, gwee-

tara Stradivarium in a floral apron
frying a ribbed glass washing board

Nice hobby, scrubbing

my country which wasn't
destroyed by war

)(

My debt as I unbind
the ice in the hinges
of the train's hair
squeaks along

Gravy baked in Go
I am making a little curtain
to protect me from the police
O Leet-el. Cur-ten. O

I love the train
I adore. I climb
the tipsy red
metal ladder I sweet

sweet needle evade
the haystack police inspector
I stare at my squaretoed suede
boots on the scarred floor

       I like the word mizz-
       er-ab-le
sez
Sonja. the fly-heart of my failed
love buzzing

from shit to food to coffee
A day in the life of

       He drew it as a flip book, very clever
          You could sell that!
she told him

)(

The swanning girls singing the names
of violated towns glister on stage
in white gowns & the football hooligans

with longing in their hearts are burning
the whole bombed city down

M is one of them. Preternaturally drunk
in sleep, sweating into dawn

& ok, let's say there is this slightly drunk
& inept person who is your soul
& slightly overweight also

Overwaiting. Filling his clothes & his rages
like a silo of drugged glass. Toasting
the golden fish & bunches of black

balloons wobbling festive
as policemen's punches slapping

down sevens then pitching forward
into nightcold panes. God of
my most adoring candor fleeing

) (

I like a gold field though
I love the absence of irony
from a life of crime

Little places just waiting
to be trashed. Gray hawk
flying swimmingly

& to trash, of an evening
The bride & bridegroom

A wing in my fit
A little bride wing, blithe wind

drunk wing sweating
horselike & hacked off
& a gold field like I said

& the blouse of the violated women
floats singing all by itself

a song about a golden fish
that doesn't make much

sense, a little banished gray
shed or banshee, a leetel
headache sweating

into the bag of loose tobacco
but no rolling paper
dawn & how bout those

how many thousands dead
& how much is
this blouse, so pretty

)(

in the creaky stranded ship of the raptor
museum a stuffed peregrine clutching a dove

reenacts an aria of defeated love. Locked
& loaded I want to float out like a bad guy's
bad white dove of fallen tree ignition

Just me and the Virgin necking
in perfect English, stroking
olive oil on each other's face & throat

to make to mask us then paper plaster &
a bandage drying suddenly tightens up. Safe
in our rages, a sturdy blue score to organize

our lives on such images of others
to record our faces so

I ~~love~~ leave Manchev yelling
affection in his language

into the stray dog's fur. I want to go out smiling
& do. Any words would spoil this

~~Seized with a fierce unreasonable love~~
~~Seized with a fiercely unreasonable love~~

~~upon departure~~ The bandaged angel
bleeding. The ex-stray dog's fur

)(˙

Gray hawk swimmingly

Bled watermelons rotting
between blown rows of corn

black sheets hung from
tree limbs, scarecrows   Nobody

today   They can't kill me
sez Igor   I have all this knowledge about them

) (

Gray-brown butteo standing
right by the tracks, thinking, officious

Gold-backed accipiter maneuvering
above watermelons

the backs of its wings
the exact color of marmalade

the exacting sadness of
hotel breakfasts

[Dear Linnaeus
what is foreign]

) (

Do you always have to make the witness
missing. I touched the back of his T-shirt
wet with his sweating into dawn

a chestnut tree dropping petals, belling
pores. What is your lifespan
exactly. The god of bread

The white of the cat's good eye
and the other a meat-socket, red
Maria-clock blinking in a dollar store

)(

[leetel hammer of departure]
against your chest & all

your cowardice & words
arrayed against it. Chilly dawn

clean as a young machine floats
toward a border. Go hang yourself

in the undestroyed tremor of a dirty pane
the famous border we're coming up on

hidden like the hunter whose sudden antlers
heralded the death of self in love

No you shut up

)(

[That all good poetry is the poetry of exile]

is bullshit, I belong to my body & try
desperately & stubbornly to unknow it

The Individual distilled into
Outspoken by Fergie

a girl on the street hands me its flyer
a naked goddess folded clutching
a giant moody purple

penis or vulva? Citizen of the new
you choose. A shell fired by
The Aggressor disrobes

revealing a fractured silver
tributary that was nothing but a line of
~~stinking women with broken teeth~~

nymphs weeping into pre-
Raphaelite hair like waterweed
~~shuffling past you, shaved~~

brown paper stained
with a little grease

)(

In and at the end
of the last La I orphaned
I, yes, the last eye ever

picking at prawns, Very pleased
to meet you Lascivious

as a trumpet festival
among a bunch of drunk
lacerations. For a nation

you have to remember words
are not a steak, pain-fed
hogs or burns hissing

from which you float upward
impossible parachute
of a drop's reversal

)(

You just adore something totally ravaged

Look at me I'm on fire. The victim-posture
a violin with burning straw for hair & bones

& safe in the sturdy bandage
we undulate to the music of worms

& isn't this a polka? Wow

) (

& now
a small white bed moving through

immensities. & what do you know
about immensities? & is it true that because

of our emotional natures women cannot write
anything truly grand? It is another white

immensity, my starched ellipsis-
trundled bed made tightly

Ok then, trundled. Now listen
although you cannot hear

Them. Immensities
The bad, & famously

unpitied, ripen

Isabella in the
Tower of Winds

This is about drowning

I'm awake.
I count that.

My sister comments
on my military coats

Chaleco Salvavidas

People look at me
as the shabby weirdo
with the notebook

Do not hold doors
Do not lean on door

I write: Will anyone
ever kiss my scar?

I grow warm with hate
for the electric Santas

Use Cable For Flotation

I think it's quizzical
(my scar) being not
perfectly straight

No loitering, soliciting, or

a sketch of hills?
but I'm not sure

the exact pursed hidden
color of angry worms

Gray wool across my shoulders.

Dollar Tree
Fish House
Red Ruby
LAW

a cervix doesn't make me
"a creature of foam"
or a high bristling ivory
collar painted in oils

ma gazzel ma gazzel
Rent A Jalopy
Mr. Junk

seen from above
beasts of burden
broadcast live

Azzo's Collision
Leo's Jewelry

I imagine uttering:
Cicatrix and straddle

scrolling through
the musical selection
red carpet and cute

little Christmas bells
Roar of engines
eclipsing lust

theorizing narratives
within the narrow

mirrored closet of
the airplane "loo"

I imagine whispering:
dripping with gems

Altitude above Sea Level
What if I had a glass clitoris?

Thank you for flying Isabella
to the horizontal green line

push flap
to grasp   plush
Isabella

the wild blue yonder.   height
every night for snowplow operations

make sure you swipe   The most
glittering rival
                         Littoral
securely fastened   Isabella
I should say, our   famous spokesanimal

Imagined grasshoppers
beget anxiety

This month we
look at the underlying

Night of travel writing: Like
everyone else I

& surely "Duty Free"
has a certain ring to
a woman kneeling

on the cover in loose blue
blowing-open armholes

Drubbed cotton
Beaten cotton
Pummeled, or what

is the word for
the more threads
the more expensive

So sad he said he wanted
to go back inside his dad's balls

Notebook Interrupted by
a Trip to the Hospital

He was a hero in their mouths / and on their chests

"and for this reason from its very foundations
this knowledge will be a thing of sand"

Oseima is diligent, mature, and extremely focused

"the original state of the mind, fresh, vast, luminous"

I am happily researching ovulation
A mafia of jinn. A caterwauling

I love this idea—the luminosity of
condemnation secretly beckons

Yes let's think about it forever

The money a holy city, a huge rusty bucket

descending / rubbing my feet
against the (wine-dark) sheets

When I read poetry I feel sad because

and from a distance—often very profitable—bask
in similitude of risk

The pull of would. That's clear
I felt how/that at the font of philosophy

Very good, very soft
very sveltely tempestuous

Sad little duck. Goat. Stone (sucked)
Slipping into fog like rabbits

My mind plastered out of I
The idea, maybe, I depend on
We discussed your fears on the bus

Her sons hold slingshots
and she hands them doves

A coughing in the margin
This is the corner I dread

and I can't bear to be with
this voice. I am simply resting

on words that make no sense
with no justification. Exit. His

Or boredom. I wallow, prissy trumpet
I got home, edited, and felt sad again

Goodnight, donkey
Dream of bare planks. Pale undressed wood

If scars are no more personal than language
The miraculous strength of hunger
Battering at what container

but this anger and coldness is not love
The factory girls. This isn't you
I is the relativizer, jealous exile gloating

Don't pray while you're drunk
from which shadow's well

It is 2 PM and I am bored
He bought stovepipe and had no money
left for food. Abject terror

yeah sure. Love me
declarative utterance
registry of overlapping earth

want and batter and antagonize
and charge. Give me a nubile yielding
form to go to him

after heartpounding jealousy and talk
I want to be selfish and pampered

in the continuous present. Broken
gatepost lion, why then

and now? Was there
no remedy for preconception?

and one candle for missing threshing tired
of waiting for him and wanting and telling

O the words. Whichever
words, unhumble. No
arm to cling to. My heart sank

because I could hear him making a myth
living halted among these colors
crooning to my solitude Thus & Therefore

This is a thought, Selah. This is a widow
in waiting and the glow of waiting
riveted to the incomprehensible

narratives that favour high-contrast
glossy salvation, dirty knives sawing
through the stems of geraniums

after dark after rain
I'm pretending I'm Hemingway

But the blocked-off street was simply
waiting. Tufted with soldiers

The country that was stolen dreams
always in the pastoral orphan

Largesse must have a proud waif to embellish it
and this refers to a symptom known as "hovering"

I am stupid with pain
Silk flowers nailed to a road

Enemies give a clear luster to winter
The water rippled, indigent

Curricula of everyday sadness
The underbellies of old cars

eaten out by salt are not silently
candelabra nor grindingly harps

If the pieta is really about [drunk on] triumph
forever if I kept crying; on Tuesday

Dust in your hair from being stepped on
Light in your face from escaping
All I know is I want warmth

An insufficient center, watching yellow leaves
Rise and fall of a chest like a book
waiting face down and open

This is an ordinary wing
A metal thing howling over oceans
The regular pleasure of
applying a salve, evenings

Blood or money. Blood
instead of apples, Robert. Repeating
the word Colorado in one poem

The damned knotted
in hell in clever paintings
I like listening to their faces

hissing. What affords this prosperity?
Everything pre-scripted, touchscreen
I too have this squeezed-out tube of Sir

Both are true—the lazy, selfish, exploitive
Birds throwing themselves at windows

like darts. Wind-packed clouds stiffly cutting
off the view of the blurred dark sea below

I want a newspaper, I want to bask
in productivity and creation

Nearly over London, between despair
and imagination I feel guilty and strange
and far and full of the glassy impossible

and unwilling to avert my gaze. I know now
the feeling of wanting to disappear
I am thinking about slaveships

This slowness is called headwinds
In the heart of the heart of
the country the shadow's question

The lambs he held still to be killed. Bashing about
in a den of insufficient wakefulness

It is a week since I was released from the hospital
There is sleeping naked except for bandages
There is planning the outfit nightly

behind closed eyes. Humans are arrayed
bored in airports, I still like guzzling
on their faces. Greedy to hold and rest on

furtively monitoring their breathing, in lieu of
credo, towards native tongue and noon

Indiscrete Leviathan

"First, the 'matter' thereof, and the 'artificer', both which is man. Secondly, 'how' and by what 'covenants' it is made ... and what it is that 'preserveth' and 'dissolveth' it."

THOMAS HOBBES, *Leviathan*

anticipate, absorb, and try to take

The encyclopedia. Its weight
as chiton. Names

rebuff reading, at least
perspective, cut-and-paste

Leviathan. The oil-on-water stately
magnifico inferno Nabokov plunge
into stiletto gush. The state as seraphim alias

razor has many guises
severally replete, immune
beige. To imagination. Blake's

Rose, lit. And bleeding sparks. Like what
shored commerce invented sparkler.

or
the Matter, Forme, & Power
of a
Common-wealth
Ecclesiasticall
and
Civill.

land which is imperishable and waters
the means of transport thence

to articulate these swift
preferences like winning

zoomed language capital I
ZED to conceive
ownership vs. pleasure's

lusciousness fallen out of
usage: whalebone, corset, stays

as the air, the wind, the spirits vital and
sometimes the images that rise in the is
nothing delivered but by the name of

under the awning of surf
brush with what can

wound would frame confession
in order to press demand

migrates between
the gathered when

my spirit at the expense of

how to break asylum to withstand
the notion of being clever

I explained the word cater and bowed
smugly with my imaginary tray

One by one I made them paraphrase
the listening on mercantilism

The parameter is annunciation, the body lifted
on a nonexistent platter toward the blind

eye of the cupola filled with cloud and gray
If we buy that

Love? what W. H. wrote about Nijinsky
or who America owns

the bones in the graveyards turned
over the names of stitches

the kinds of orchards the pastoral
lacquering the stolen to which

it is always at heart
dramatizes a total

I don't want to be stranded
even through a wound
                              —the orderly
crouching beside my belly and coaxing
off the bandages (forth from the little telling

hairs) so very gently and saying sorry   sorry
sorry   for their stickiness
                              —where
does kindness come from and can you notice
that you contain bones?

I I I in the green tiled walls
of my highschool phonebooth with the font

getting smaller as I type this
culpable as Alice—   knowing

a fish by the crunching of its bones. Its little lyric bones

Did the water all boil away yet? Dizziness
In the middle of a dark wood the wish for

a beginning breaking

but I cannot not
exist again yet
crouching in

a furnace squatting
prim as grass
ground glinting

objects within
it seem not

radiant shades
into overarching

end, fungible

burst of If,

Blurbing the Reconquista

Oum Kulthum's voice tearing itself apart
armaments of flesh carnations

The stewardess stepping down the dark
aisle like a fugue repeating

The taste of clay in clawed trenches
a wall of applause forty years old

banned, obscene, immensely profitable
the word water in three languages

I imagine I'm the fucking Irish
banging trashcan lids Police
Police! against smutty sidewalks

while actually music lets rue in
to my chest to get crushed there
where a wreath of plucked grass

stems begets stars. My listening
nipples wistful arsonists. Will
I ever own a complete set of towels

Would that every house had fallen
in around my stuffed howl. I imagine
someone's mouth on my breasts ·

(first the left) just for something to do
on this aer-o-plane, this lady's elbow
keeps touching my elbow, I don't want to

grow bright again with loneliness, this spotlight
only stark because no one else can see by it
Or gnaw on. That night he was crying

under the trellis, our backs to the cold
cheap trailer he resented paying rent for
I guess a pyre could be asylum but not

for whom. Wet-faced to the straggling ivy
hiding some form of moon. About how dry
and calloused his father's hands and feet are

Burgeoning with sleep I think
whose net is this cast upon the pearlescence
and is it monitoring my heartbeat

At the center is not being
able to breathe. I couldn't sleep

and so discovered a genre (Welsh)
called "exultation." Night
on the black windows of "The Swan"

3 tallskinny girls in white short shorts
(just before Trafalgar Square) ignite in me
the strong wish to smell like strawberries

and a scream budding from my chest
like breasts. Something that takes a long time
to recognize. Then wistful arson

Passing the night-dull statue
of the famous rider, inside me

an incredible privacy still reigns. Stealth
I thought was ardor

To almost die within sight of the sea
is normal (hurled herself

from) Race or ethnicity
as stain, the moon

darling is a distant train
never getting closer

A hammer at the façade
of an unseen building

studs listening. Blood in
volute flanges, fingers

to count beads. The highest
passes into which they withdrew

to be defeated. These silvers
so bereft in me, neglected creases

could be posh. You means other
people I don't really see

ascent scrolled escalating into floor
-to-ceiling glass Airtrain
station two flamingo streaks flank

the sootifying skyline, New Jersey
is unreal / I imagine

retelling my favorite sections of The Odyssey
What is prose? When I don't have this feeling
of wanting to destroy anything so strongly

Cargo Area depthless
charcoal / I described the body

returned from the hospital still
with two bullet holes and the new gash
opened diagonally from shoulder to hip between

What does bombed-out mean? Like plum trees
a genre of sequence. The figures of buildings

newly scalloped and pocked edges
O Jen we ate shit / O Jenfer
The doors are closing, please hold on

There is a brief sweetness at least
to opposing any overwhelming structure

And this our courted and made-up
constellation. I like the shape of
my name with some letters missing

A new compact sculpted by blows
Nymph as windlass. Like fiera (beast)

leads toward Inferno merged with people
surging forward like wheat deliberately
chanting the names of cities. What is shame?

Long padded bags with little gold wheels
like bells at one end, people are dragging them

across the shiny floor towards running
belted machines. A little plaid to protect
their hidden nested skis. The next flight

to Geneva / O Jen we

The Dead Girl

Type with your eyes closed: The dead girl. The dead girl. 14 is what you heard at first but Google turns up 13, 13, Hala Hala Something. Shot in the back at a school protest. Is the second name same as the first a typo? How do scholars spend years writing books about books?

+

Imagine someone writing the word "protest" on a black- or whiteboard. The order of letters, a list of terms. Say to yourself, you are a teacher of English, you convey fixed rules, forgetting also must have a syntax as inconspicuous as the body continuing, nostalgia stuck billowing, ditto homeostasis, eros as identification, distraction that sustains and saves us. Is this why I have to massage the scar, so the layers of flesh don't stick together forever, creating a wooden soldier at last at least?

+

Government, state, power, forces, security: refer to what? A game of chess? I can't remember how any of the pieces move, except the one that can pounce in a prim swift L. I need to do laundry, I wish someone would lift my forehead off gently and set it on a pedestal like a reconstructed antique vase. I want a label also, affixed to the white wall next to me. White letters on white on white. The writing is just to bind the whites fast. Behind my back. The game is over when no one (else) can move.

A hapless brightness intrudes regularly, and battered taxis circle dingy roundabouts anchored with statues, weave around each other like bottom feeders, circadian, trapped. What has consequence here is linear trajectory, a formerly cloistered vector multiplied and spent, a handful of empty brass and the tactile pleasure of letting held shells drop at random. Whereupon, wherein, whereby, whereas, he refused to look at and fled from. My body's textbook cut, mirror mirror, unclotting rev of engines, eyesight is forming as gluts of cells divide and divide again, sheering from ago and thence, not yet garnered by fright—

+

Emotion which spends itself on subjectivity, thou-fraught abundance, sure, cash in hand, one's breath in tandem with another, another's, or conscripted within the scope of audiovisual recording devices into singing No One Is A Liar to oneself, since how much of the surface of the terrestrial earth is being remotely monitored at this second, thus the dead girl, therefore the dead girl, whereupon redundant pixels broadcast through a night, while local to a few rooms only, the smells of people who once touched her and some even made her cry.

+

Here blind as glue, my thinking growing cataracts. Here glowing drunkish blue for who must dwell in awareness of helplessness: the dead. Girl, a clasp you fumble with, no one to put that necklace on for you, to manage the chain's cool drape behind your back, me, I am here still feeling, no need to rewind and play back. Breath falling on your hair unfelt, unfeeling, the texture of most wood you touch is actually that of varnish or lacquer.

I am interested in supplementing my own smells.
I am applying to my wound oil and honey.
Christ, a knife, a bird carved from green wood. The word life

+

The words stuck behind the forehead with brainfog of sad calories can't. Rend
your tents God said or something like that. I don't have a tent, someone cut
open my belly instead. Now I smear a little honey on that place, evenings.
Then suck the rest off of my finger. I like the taste, like time continuing. To go.
To the color of worms paling, stretched thinner exerting themselves towards
disappearing into wet earth. A letter once you learn to write it in cursive
disappears into the tendons of your hand and wrists, a theater quarantined by
instinctive lacunae and that pretty much sums up victory, thanks.

+

One day when he came to my bed and lay down in it he said they gave the
body back yesterday and he said the name but I didn't know it and forgot. It
had lines down it—the body—cuts, black, down the chest, they had had it for
weeks, opened and kept. I said I don't understand why they would give it back
like that, don't they want to hide it, what happened. What they did. You don't
understand he said, or maybe he didn't. I still don't.

But I liked the thing clipped to my fingertip: like a clothespin-turned-
irradiated-cave, it was sucking my pulse onto a TV screen with the blind
doggedness of sunflowers crossbred with lasers, a little green line, a field of
hummocked graves, oscillation, wavelength, Blake attacking the sky with
the tip of his umbrella, Chaplinesque and better off at least than Oedipus or
Lear blind yet still challenging the parameters of their stiff helplessness with
speech—

+

And the weird slick heat when they pulled out the stint—from friction, I
guess—felt like a hot worm plucked from my belly. Undone in a trice. By the
milk of human kindness plus or minus what we are capable of making. One
pleasure of being we is uttering it, my job is just to fix the grammar, this may
hurt a little, but it is not in our best interests to rush me, thanks.

+

I am also the Viking in the 9th century carving his name into the upper banister
of the Hagia Sophia, hailing inside a symphony or the Pacific the instinct to
play ditto, pull out a knife and start hacking away into whatever armrest, Igor
was here. Ribs, or what are known as ranks of men, candle flicker, a zipper
keeled open with zzzzzz, sounds like armed to the teeth, might love me.

Naming the rampant new melting jellyfish sun after a John Donne poem was
a good one, though what genius nursed on helplessness could have done
otherwise, O wilderness of cells pierced with light? They could see the bones
in their forearms through their closed eyelids because they raised their arms
to cover their faces, of course thought courses toward shelter through cadence,
predictable, even predatory when incredulity is also a kind of mental armor
and even dressing has to be relearned—For DNA, read half-life.

+

Between bouts of typing I smooth pink worms of eyecream from a tube under
my eyes and above them. Watching in a mirror, with one eye then the other.
With mortality too there are procedures and this comfort often guarantees
that dictators are somewhat loved just as my fingers know where all the
letters are without any reason or scrutiny involved. Please use reasons and
details to support your answer. I for example like to organize an avalanche for
example with just tympanums and synapses firing, hushed white, new powder
lifting from the windshield's brightness, for example acceleration wind and
blindness, plus a keyboard for percussion, made in China or wherever.

+

I cringe shut all my fringes like a black jellyfish asterisk deleted inwards against
any loss i.e. touch, I depress a button, a screen glows, Select a Power Plan:
(selected) : * Balanced

Via of against:

+

I will mention the dead girl and thus be noble. I am shit or maybe worse
he said giving me his usual excuse for fleeing. Then fled. Flesh of my flesh.
Unscramble the nadir untwist the coded saturnalia twirling a glassy morning
glory down the drain with inertia's gagging suck. You emerged also dragging a
fleshy cord smeared with blood after you, and after: this game of telephone
ending in limbs and cicatrix, uprooted candle flicker, you, victor, salve your
binding nonesuch with which so-called native tongue?

+

I am applying honey to my wound. From Athenian pines. No joke. Every
night, I smear a careful smile glistening sidelong. Then I suck my fingertip and
talk to you out loud. No no no, how could you—

Like applying glue for a fake moustache backstage of a vaudeville skit I follow every night, I am starting to like the taste of honey as a habit. The tidiness of the taped bandage. White belly-moustache, a kind-faced bland bachelor. And your absence.

+

Tonight I hope to dream I am a whale. Belle of Leviathan. For tulle, Hiroshima. For huge, read sad.

+

Hala Hala, in Beirut I looked at pictures my friend showed me on YouTube of people releasing hundreds of paper lanterns into the sky, its night just fallen. They rose, somehow floating. Somewhere in Poland. I thought at first it was just white shapes painted on the deep blue walls of a hotel ballroom. Then I understood the walls were a life I had imagined and would not ever have or have to leave as others touched my skin with their trying hands. No such sea partitioned, nor to be parturated in advance, nor could be. My heart is really beating but it is meaningless to say so. Thanks.

Wartime Garden

My Name Is Raji

How can I put a tank in a poem

I picture a Ferris wheel on its side
insects proliferating under the sky

Why attach to drama, a little red funding

like a balloon bobbing upward from my wrist
making onward movement auspicious
& awkward at once. Hello pale worried sailor

tacking up a curtain against the sun. I smell hot
spilling candle. Throw a dime against the sky
a new monster flowers up the water boiling

There was other equipment also the taxi driver knew
& had been specialized in & explained excitedly

But they just put them there to scare people
he added, they never use them

The next shot shows a traveler slowly rising
from where he had been sitting leaning against a wall

It is about tiredness & love. Stars behind brown cloth
imaginary & real at once. Time passes. It is in fact
a tablecloth flapping, stained with candle wax

My name is Raji. Do you like tanks? Where are you from?

Virgin vs. Non-Virgin Ghazals

Who is so lovely I can't look at him
& not write poems. He Who Sings Ghazals
About Farting. Shut up or I'll cook you

he tells the cold caged bulbuls puffed-up
like travelers in expensive parkas cooing
whose ballroom waltz whose vault whose trigger

whose welcome mat of grass cropped close
parching the soft white roots of pity
from everyone under it equally

like drunkenness of tossed quicklime
mirth-twist of mouth just giving over
to weeping. Uncloseable lidless eye

is God? I imagine telling him: then there was
the bullfighter lifted from the dust
by both elbows, his face swinging

from just left of where it used to hang
like a staid locket portrait of Emerson dizzied
by eternity in prodigal early American landscapes

unburying his dead first wife. Roll on, columbaria
my love has memorized this one sentence
in English: Sarajevo is a catless city.

In any world I am a sucker, I carol smeared
on my own glass slide. Open-mouthed

in sleep he / Bones & all

I want this never to finish

The School of Gypsy Fountains

& here was the gorgeous rose
-blat of his mouth
on my fright. Stood awake

scion-narrow behind my closed
eyelists listening night

permeable vaudeville of worry's
watercolor bleeding out. His seedheart
ticking in his cake-tin skinniness

He is imagining water, flowers, lamps
I want a necklace of huge bear teeth
& a flowing bearskin

into which to sink naked
purblind intractable self-hatred
achieving drunkenness

even greater than this
flight unfought or sated

+

Unbird my debt my dart
my dark slow-witted

constellation turning rooted
palinode the castled space

between the choosing
of each word in the chain

of subordinates the layout
a functional retina threads

of water flowing down
through the old walls

the seven layers of heaven
I will not mention here

any of his parts or graces

+

One arm a foundling in vendetta
against sleep. Sure there were pines
in my childhood, my ear licks the pages

turning crowns the lap of luxury
with the king's creaking, I was three cracked
lamps shone in his delirium but he

putting his arms around us all
on permanent death/beauty patrol
I lick yr beard, suck in my stomach

Who photographs himself smoking
wrinkles his brow practicing curses
in the sex of evening new & unknown

Your sister on the cocks of a hundred horses
Unobserved withal I was the glow
of bruised fruit aging furious in a bowl

+

Exhale. My hair uncurried linden
ocean dressing the frail green insect
of his body's brief convulsion

I chop up the peach anyway
& the knife keeps finding
the stone, the stone

I drink the milk of the story
of him beaten with his fancy new shoes
blinking for loving them too much stepping

so carefully watching him touch
each of the new plant crowns & thinking
He Who Walked Neatly Home

Airy Dregs

I like the new hot weight of my wet clothes
& hang them rustling too quickly. Evil forest
cut throat breathing of the yet-kicking

I keep getting quietly drunk on fear
because a captive is important. He shrugs

& bursts into a bird of flame
& chases three spiders unclenching
crawling back into their airy dregs

to start again. To be anyone else
even the moon, the kid eating chalk
in the corner—in the closet

surrounded by other rank skins
than hers—for even punches
are a kind of applause—

I want to polka with him
in a mythical grove

My hairy messy house
with ferocious insect corners

& I the wicked brother killing whatever
to outdo sadness with malice
& I wish I were black iron

for any hand to warm. Love enters
at 14 holding a lamb steady
for the older man's knife

& through his fingers flows
the ebbing pulse. He maniacally apes
the same death raveling ignition

in every throat, the parching ivy
still straggling up waving its 1,000
tiny mirrors. Water-reflections

shatter up from the center
of a terrible garden. Hair & breath
Pleasure of normal millions

Fake Boat

I press my face into the dark boat
of my cupped palms leaking
from the central seam like the King

of Sadness smelling everything he cuts
to get to his own keel line. Only
he doesn't like his own XXX

Don't write about this. He writes

My fingers trembling like the sacrifice
sprout leaves/My breaths competing
with the louder roar cheering

the executioner: by what right do I touch you
high in the last blue in the back & forth
twittering desolation that chews the air

They have decided on the violence
surrounding women inventing new faces
of strenuous calm in public mirrors

in the stupor of the third day of shelling
work, go home, eat, watch TV, sleep
if they kill 100,000. Lion lion

HOW TO MINUET. The skein of prayer-calls
blurs out over the city. As usual sadness
in the architecture of the stairs

They stretch the holy name out
like mourners washing a body
Firmament & cucumbers

& are the whores still working. Probably
even better. The king of sadness
opens his mouth to catch a moth

& we laugh about knowing
what kind of bullet killed his cousin
Next to the bus station in wet sea air

Each of our bodies formed & was routinely
carried that under the bulldozer sea of
summer now duly we abound

Now Duly We

I asked him to bring me a stone
He brought me seeds

Every day I climb up
a litter of failed objects

playing cards: 2 of beasts
jack of hearts, sacrifice
w/ a flood of water
hair from stars

My country from a distance
all power chords. A whole
generation floats past
the nada mark speechless

underwater. I've failed
to be the perfect plastic doll
buried naked in the dirt

these 20-cent plants keep
their white roots in needing
besides only a little light & water

I want to hide in its darkness
through the time it takes to wash
the blood from the streets

There are machines for this
I don't know how to drive them

Embedded Pastoral Curse

The style of this poem is
I'm A Little Dictaphone

LD: Wake & face a screen
Screen: metallic soundings

from gray swirling. Deep brink of metal
things traveling through. Light
is a wavelength too

What holds the household intact
Is it primarily visible or not

gravity root system retina sparkplug fire
dire little goodnight hug

Unless the pigeon's wings are your
hands & feet tapping. Escape
through the ceiling?

Someone is still wearing his orphan
for pajamas. Swish of

the window willow's dusty green
forlorn someone

should sweep & wash the floor
someone should grit her teeth

& draw her sword
& refuse to tell a story

What Happens on the Moon

The strawberries finished the apricots begun
the cracked ridged thumbs of the Armenian tailor
now permanently drunk are two miniature black whales

dried tough from being dragged along a broad pale beach
no one knows where. The moon's beach? No one
knows. The moon rests its creased forehead

on piles of other people's exhausted clothes
& when I close my eyes white crossed bars
of windows hover before dark diamonds, wet cliffs, gulls

cry drifting. My marrow curdles phosphorescent
with shame we trees winter back to belly & turn
again candled & sinking gnats above the meatfisted hole

in the new corpse's waxy neck. Puppets with their strings
cut a tiny larch a minnow a little tissue. You shovel
a spoonful of gritty honey in your cigarette-mouth, suck

the two-fingered muzzle of your "gun" laughing at the bright
burp of blood it would flatten like a red lampshade
on the clean white wall behind the sofa. I bang, I gain & dim

What happens on the moon is none of my business.

Soliloquizer

Light comes & goes.

You grow a new beard
& your friend follows suit

You long for a gun in your hand
to possess consequence
not to crouch in a hole

All words fail me & I fail
to hold any clear shape
or certain knowledge

I want to do something worth lilies
& nosebleed, eating shawarma

You come back across mountains
& fix the washing machine

Radio melismas burn
the freshly dead ignored

I hang wet sheets in the new night
& smell their darkened red

Damascus

"If the countries less rich than ours have at their disposal at least one tank per citizen, then for us as Arabs, with all the endless wealth and resources God has given us, there must be not just one but five tanks at least for each citizen:

one on his right,
one on his left,
one in front of him,
one behind him,
and one on top of him.

And thus he relaxes and makes someone else relax."

MOHAMMAD AL-MAGHOUT, *I Will Betray My Country*

Dime-Store Travelogue

Someone lifted a strand of my hair & smelled it
& I began my travels

through oranges & rain. & the dark wood
of my own scarred table. I thought there
should be a castle around my voice

but there were only two roosters sprouting
their wish to be roses & the holy blood of the slain
into the sound of water cunningly unbuckling

a spider played her alphabet against
my tympanum making a charm
for my fingernails to stay rooted

in their beds like the royalty of women
who sold themselves kept deep in their minds
while skin simpled & stuttered yes

I am a good audience & by this evade detection
& disgrace. Maybe you didn't notice
me crouching, a marvelous villa inside a slave

The city not yet in flames. For an hour
erase naught with if. Because it is
the stronger thing we must prevent ourselves from

imagining until the hour of our deaths
so as not to know how strongly we exist

Dear Dead

Walter B. please walk
with me on your arm

through the waylaid memory
of broken glass & oily flames softening

these chestnuts roasting, small white brains
translating the sounds of us in bedsheets

as they break open & my hand moving
across the page. To be stunned

Make a whole sentence please.

My little rat-footed soul tasted the dirty fleece
collar of his jacket as he eyed the ground.

The Turks threatened to reveal
their penises at the dinner table.

"We are practical people."

The mode of address here is the crux
Fasces > carried by lictors

Torches—think white electric larches
Closeness: like the crowd in Canetti

burning only to grow & tear
down all barriers to its growth

To pry an object from its shell

to destroy: lost aura of
early portraiture of

the face
Arditi. I love this word

& longed to put my soul in

someone else's mouth so
he could speak me

Into the furnace of
opal ridicule   *but*

the human need for shelter

On the ferry deck
smelling the water & trying

to perceive against the beauty of fires

The Derivation of the Word Sultan

in the light of our romancia knowledge
another country hopes & stalls. Why
that most useless of silk palaces

Maybe I have built castles to men & doubt
You invented a judge & so surrounded
yourself with a thousand mirrored walls

He is writing from the point of view of a woman
I wasn't dealt another card

I wish for fluency & divide into imagining
the skeleton inside each passerby
The prisoner observing other prisoners

Circulation from sea to clouds
to something oaken grained
with lightning-rasped char

To focus light
To pour out fire

shapes spreading in smoke
like skeins of light
thrown from moving water

In the sour dark the sound of dripping water
placed a small flame in my throat

in the nave of the boat
in the ship's ribbed galley

I wished for you to take off your shirt
& reluctant to sleep stood guard
on the threshold of an imagined power

which never arrived, stashed in a blush
that no longer makes me sordid
Bored w/ description. Too soft

I sequester myself on the quietest day
(Sabbath tailored w/ several darts)

& the dead emerge about midday
like time-lapse flowers, crystals of salt

Don't let them see you have a camera
& if they find it say it's broken
Our eyes. Formed from a sea, bored

behind the future. In the hospitals
how many wounded & how many
vowels elided & buried together

severed from names. Draw another
line, begin. Again differently

not to falter, but. To drown, queued quietly
waiting to be videoed crossing a border

The Dream of the Fountain

Holding hands suddenly through the thieves'
market of cheapest vegetables & phones
posits a renegade voice elicited against

exhaustion. The curve of
a woman's back at the bar, tall
yellow lights ranked warmly behind her

Woman, curving forward
too far—forced harp, fake child

& did we not curtsey
before the huge black breath
we dared not draw, of air that tickles leaves

& surrounds dwarves precisely
& sweeps pollen from the glass faces

of office buildings far from this dust-streaked
concrete backstage of old men's conversation
over cards, wind from the desert rustles

the severed wings of never-stars
My body swimming in sea air unfamiliar

safety gray dropsical then brilliant
& full of ordinary cars.

+

The Stranger. White mercury scythe-
gleam, scant meniscus of
day trembling in the emptied glass

You appear at my door ready to flee
& deny you were ever there

or we are careful toward each other, expensive
jewelry arrayed in a broad glass case

I want only to eat & dream & remember
& see & be quiet

Outside the gallery sheltering
nubbled canvases of exiles
I touch the flat surface of the fountain

which is the dream of the coin
with no face no raptor no
monument no figure

only the new skin
over a burn foreign

primaeval interior welling
refusal to disappear

+

Where is this voice from
How well & easily the body knows danger

molds to it & fits together inwardly
like white plastic mannequins
into operatic postures of abandonment

How bones can be broken
How sea-foam popping slowly on sand
How a circus tent is taken down
after the licked fingers of the event

starting with the toes the pegs the traces
the shadow the fingernail
clippings the gritty dregs

starting with the vague white drifty torn
end of the bitten thread

Each fear christens a new wax museum
catalogue & antagonists, chrysanthemums
men's eyes my failure at seamlessness

lungs & shoulders plunged from sleep
city trees edged with motions streaming repeated
pleated rushes rooted & pulled downstream
How much & luckily selfishness simplifies

yet   I can't feel my way forward with language
yet   tongue towards the brink
yet   let what is unknown elate me

a new lover smelling my ear
a woman demanding of her own ribs
a boat grown from a candle, from the modest flame
something hitherto unknown now pleasing

Thank You James Blunt for Your Input

The last song is dropping hot glass knobs
petaling globby onto my bare knees
bookless & tucked up, I'm tired from teaching

verbs, especially. Late song I mean hast been
giving me the creeps. The creep, thou
[injury: see, father] cursed the idiot floating

candles drifting into the shower-curtain-fountain
-liner with green rosebuds squatting on a grid
like bored executive frogs unburned

not even singed & I want something more
molten suicide interior of the sun lost
Alhambra & Arabs mourning for 5 centuries

if they haven't been arrested in the last two days
& if they are not beaten into revealing
country-shapes never really invented

except on their skins, & not exactly that blue
that is my favorite, but more green
or red, like your shoulders and broken

bicycle underfoot, & under clubs also
in my sympathetic literary fantasy
the fifth tank glistens over me like a giant

lilypad if lilypads were hot metal ticking
& I was a soft tiny frog like I wanted
to show you in the shower, & clever, also

by thou poets often mean I but not
always. & I swear by all this damage
enjambment vs. joints, no contest

Odysseus Wept

Come unto me bald little tortured doll
Come unto me broken toy
robot, necessary subjects

boot-heels clacking on parquet
small patterns still dutifully marching
across the children's blouses

in the museum display in this painting
regular rows of pastel dots floating
before faces play the past intervening

in seeing. All those Russian peasants
must be killed. The famous old man swearing
to God on camera *I can't remember*

how to form a sentence. Every time he starts a novel
The peasants wanted money, how banal
they were to be alive at all in the thirties

Now just as a war starts people watch it
on TV. Today it was a frame around gray
dust rising & swirling down

from a great height. You face a screen
emitting metallic beeps. You could spend years
weaving museum labels for each image

from your own hair. *Sand That was Buildings*
for example or *There Must be Dogs Left There?*
or *Odysseus Wept to the Song Called 'Odysseus*

Raping the Steep City'. You could start a novel
from the point of view of a lamb who can't wake
from dreaming her throat is being cut. People are happy

to own smaller & smaller objects that play music
& choosing the music they want to play
You can put a picture on it

& change the picture. Over & over
it is very easy & so they do
& are. The name of this song is

Even When I'm Betraying You I Miss You

Gaping Queen

I watch the breaths of strangers raising
their pale shirts & shoulders. The last thing
I have kept from church: people to rest on
without them seeing. My liege

I would be a line of castles above a sea
a dismantled enemy evident in a stone
remnant of their thinking, clean

while it's impossible to name this present
night-city except by smells: dirt & shit
after rain. In the morning we turn on the TV
to see if the number of dead has risen

Why not say killed? I wish to inhabit
just for five minutes
the strides of the ones with guns

say sunder say Magellan, the space between
the thunder & the root, the tongue-gleam
& the waxy comb crawling with bees

only six today last week nearly a hundred
In the candle-flicker I count
like graphing the curve of a string

of amber beads lifted from the decaying
ribs & collarbones of a gaping

queen. Her crumbling a rare cage
for something brief & taken

& I obeyed, I did not move—

Dispatch

I explain error, errand, chivalry (errant)
utopia, ropes in sand. Of sand. The King
(of Sadness): unconvinced

his semen is "like an ocean." Semen, slightly
unlike oceans. Photograph (mine): light
on his profile from thin candles he lit & stuck

in a line. Caption: THE VERY YOUNG
[MEN], THEIR CHEEKBONES
GLISTEN. My old student Jeff in California
bringing me diagrams of missiles'

explosive yields, glossy pink & turquoise
concavities like airbrushed lampshades. For pitching
a cartoon about shy pudgy creatures & their singing

lives under the sea. So softly surely singing
Bob's poem about California, plums. Thus
what I'm thinking about, skinning kiwis: balls

General Dynamics, noses molybdenum
& softer silver. Sheep in Afghanistan
pastured on mountainsides to troll for missiles

Milling nightlong wearing lanterns. ALL MEMBER
STATES IN GOOD FAITH. I explain forbidden
bidding, abide. All bidden all rise

all headshot headlong sunlight. I buy
& offer sponges, conceal my flinches
though I also stroke them, colorful plumage

to fletch my Moi, exotica rising silky from the mud
& streets with blood washed off or ground in
with a road grader if there's too much

I explain the word inspire   [to breathe in spirits]
I wish I had more evil in me, just to feel strong & safe
continuous exhalation   A handful of empty goldish casings

Imagination making: how the bullets spun
Cannot picture the city with its nice round million
Water hisses heating in its mottled cylinder

My friends in California memorizing finches
Is it accurate to say "hemmed with tanks"? Or
is "hemmed in" better? & I the dark eyes

in the bark slashed where lopped branches
would hide in this tree from the bang
of a door. Can't erase. The other.

Now. After the first gush
of astonishment, this ugly mixture

Warden of the corolla of my mind
Let me crack the safe
Like the body shot through the eye

What do you expect to see in a face
How to exist outside of words

I confuse the words for *back* & *shadow*
We can identify the hero by his scar

Postcard to the Angel Jibreel

Day after day fires & as people favor visuals
reasons peter out. There is nothing holy
says the king of sadness. A jester like Jesus
daubing his face with tears of wine

A wound I misrecognized for a long time
as my own mother salving herself
by feeding us & crying. Thus I envy breakage

being all good posture & pantomime
& can smell the cheap beer sweated
from my blush. Sometimes

a shy bear, adamantine
Clementine of thumbs
White gravy on biscuits
Dust kicked up by big trucks

I want to be smaller than a comma
tenacious, some new unnamed virus
Maybe it never gets named. Nothing
said the king & drank bleach

& no angel came forth with seven wings
(*Uh cool can I touch it?*) Just puke
ate his teeth & vindictive ghosts of fish
fin piratical through his thinned intestines

The meek sprinkle baby powder in the wave-
prints of the president's guffaws, I pout
muttering at the edge of the historic
conflagration (*to club, to trample*)

In the new footage some of the bodies sit up
grudgingly like circus animals' understudies
(*to kick also*—) O balloon face, puffy

with fortune's purples, the waterwheel turning
spills its narrowed silvers. With my fingers
I daub wine around the king's small nipples

Distant City

I'd be on a hillside singing
my nun-arms outstretched

My liege. Alive in words we don't use
I descend cracked stairs to buy sponges

submerging from a blue line of hills. Whose lyric
distance cleverly shifted the place of fighting

to fuzzed clicks on the phoneline. We are circling
quietly on a gray tether of an unknown length

of time. Can I picture the ones striding
with guns & things like cobweb

-slingshots for electricity
Not really. Do not make a slim body a god

of diffidence. Though I fear pleasure
& that I contain many errors

starting with architecture for hiding women
I tell you about the green forest

of my youth, the men who tipped me
Each morning we turn on the TV to see

if the death toll's changed, already bored
with numbers. Image petitioning

the chambers of memory: a body lolling
rusty on a street's smeared yellows

Your beautiful arm-sinews
Did you not tell me not to move

& then daub honey
on my forehead & breastbone, my belly & belly

in the sign of the enemy, in its form of blessing
like designing a louche new form of frailty

a green insect twinkling thready
to conjure thoughts of crushing it

Florid & petty, the murderer & the bloodied
A distant city of honey, lit with globes of honey

Acknowledgments

Thank you to the editors of the following publications where many of these poems first appeared: *A-Minor, Country Music, Drunken Boat, Esque, Fence, Finishing Line, Forklift Ohio, Greatcoat, Handsome, InDigest, Poets for Living Waters, Quarterly West, Shampoo, Softblow, Transom, Typo,* and *Word for/Word.*

Thank you Ric Bowdy, Annie Dillard and F. D. Reeve for the tutelary kindness, and G. C. Waldrep for the patient, careful reading. Huge thanks to my mother Jill and my sister Heather for mailing out manuscripts while I stayed far away, and to Rebecca Wolff for seeing this one through. Thanks most of all to 3mo, for the first garden and everything after.

FENCE ⊒ BOOKS